MARIA TALLCHIEF

By Marion E. Gridley

DILLON PRESS, INC.
MINNEAPOLIS, MINNESOTA

©1973 by Dillon Press, Inc. All rights reserved
Second printing 1975

Dillon Press, Inc., 500 South Third Street
Minneapolis, Minnesota 55415

Printed in the United States of America

Library of Congress Cataloging in Publication Data

Gridley, Marion Eleanor, 1906-1974
  Maria Tallchief.

  (The Story of an American Indian)
  SUMMARY: A biography of the Osage Indian girl who
became a world-renowned ballerina.
  1. Tallchief, Maria—Juvenile literature.   [1. Tallchief,
Maria. 2. Dancers] I. Title. II. Series.
GV1785.T32G74   792.8'2'0924   [B] [92]   73-8382
ISBN 0-87518-060-4

MARIA TALLCHIEF

By the time Maria Tallchief achieved world renown
as a ballerina, the hard work and heartbreaks
along the way had tempered her strong talent in
such a way that her performances were unforgettable
to all who saw her dance. Born in 1925 in Fairfax,
Oklahoma, her father was a full-blooded Osage.
Her Scotch-Irish and Dutch mother was a strong
influence on Maria and her younger sister, Marjorie.
The two girls worked hard on their music and
dance lessons as children, and sometimes performed
together. At seventeen, Maria left home to join the
Ballet Russe. More years of dedication and hard
work, and strength in the face of disappointment,
followed before Maria Tallchief earned a lasting place
in the history of dance as one of the world's
greatest ballerinas.

Contents

CHAPTER I

People of the Middle Waters

Many years ago, in the eighteenth and nineteenth centuries, there was an Indian tribe living along the lower Missouri River known as the Osage. The Osage Indians were one of the largest and most important of the midwestern tribes.

It is believed that the Osage Indians originally came from the Piedmont area of Virginia. Later they moved to lands along the Ohio River, until pressures from surrounding tribes in some long ago period forced them farther westward to the lands along the Missouri. Here, their villages lay between the Spaniards to the south, the French on the Mississippi, and the English along the Wisconsin River.

Osage legends tell a different story about where the Osage people came from. The Osage, they say, were once spirit beings who lived in the lowest of four worlds. Two of these worlds were above the earth, the earth was the third world, and the fourth was below the earth.

One day these beings made their way to the highest world. There they were given souls by Wa-kon-da, the supreme power. Then they returned to the lowest world, to settle in a red oak tree. From its branches the people found their way to earth as men.

In another version of the legend, the Osage people were at one time sent down from the stars to live upon the earth. There they met another group of people who were of the earth. The two became one, and called themselves Osage, the "People of the Middle Waters."

The Osage were a deeply religious people. They believed that Wa-kon-da was the giver of all life. He lived everywhere and within everything. Every morning and evening the people prayed to Wa-kon-da. Many ceremonies of thankfulness to Wa-kon-da were held throughout the year.

For a long time, the Osage were a farming people. They had large cornfields and they also raised pumpkins, squash, beans, and potatoes. They gathered wild plants, berries, grapes, and several kinds of nuts. They hunted for deer, turkey, and prairie chickens with fine bows made from a tree known as the Osage orange tree. But the most important game of all was the buffalo, which they hunted in the summer and fall. They depended on the buffalo for both meat and skins.

The Osage were a tall people, taller than most of the tribes around them. The men were often over six feet tall. Their houses were made of a hickory sapling framework with straight walls, covered with mats or buffalo skins. One cabin-like hut was often thirty to one hundred feet long and was occupied by several families.

After the Osage came in contact with the Spanish and French, their old customs and ways began to change. Both Spain and France wanted to gain control of the New World, so they competed with each other to win the friendship and loyalty of the Osage Indians. They were the first tribe in the Midwest to be given guns by the French. From the

Spaniards they obtained horses. With guns and horses, the Osage tribe became strong and powerful and played an important part in the development of the New World.

Life now became easier for the Osage in many ways, too. For example, horses allowed them to travel long distances. They began to depend almost entirely on hunting for their food, leaving the gardens to the care of the old people. The hunters and their families would travel together in search of game, then come back to the villages for the fall harvest.

When hunting, the people lived in tipis made of poles set in a conical shape and covered with tanned hides. These tipis were designed to be put up and taken down quickly and easily. The poles could be lashed together to form a drag pulled by a horse, which was used when traveling to carry household belongings.

When the French explorer and missionary Father Marquette first visited the Osage in 1673, he recorded that the people wore clothing of animal skins. Skins were made into moccasins, leggings, and breech cloths for the men, and moccasins and simple dresses for the women. In the winter, the men added a leather shirt for warmth. Their hair was shaved to a strip on top called a roach. Sometimes they wore caps of beaver or otter fur. In cold weather, the people wrapped themselves in buffalo robes. Both men and women tattooed their bodies.

From the early French and English traders the Osage obtained metal kettles for cooking, traps for hunting, steel needles, thread, colored ribbons, beads, and colored yarns. Clothing was now made of cloth and trimmed with ribbons cut into small designs and stitched to the material. Belts

Osage Indians
in traditional dress

were woven from the yarns. The beads were used for embroidery and weaving, or fashioned into necklaces. Shawls and blankets replaced the buffalo robes.

The Louisiana Purchase of 1803 was to have a great effect on the future of the Osage tribe. In this purchase, the newly formed nation of the United States bought 800 thousand square miles from the French — the whole western half of the Mississippi Valley, including the lands on which the Osage were living. The Osage had always been friendly to the Americans, and they peacefully agreed to cede their lands to the United States and move to a reservation in Kansas.

It wasn't long, however, before white settlers began to cross the Mississippi in large numbers. They spilled out over the prairies and flowed around the Indians living there. The Kansas lands of the Osage were especially desirable. It was good soil, fertile and perfect for farming. The Indians put it to little use, cried the settlers, and they stood in the way of opening up the West. The country could not grow unless something was done about them.

The government eventually yielded to pressure from the settlers. Land was selected and set aside as Indian Territory in what is now Oklahoma. At that time, it was land nobody wanted. Indians were urged to move there, and if they refused, they were forcibly taken there.

The Osage saw that they would have to move. What could a few Indians do against the government? They agreed to sell their Kansas holdings and go to Indian Territory. In 1871, with the money from the sale of their lands, the Osage bought a million and a half acres for their new home in the northeast part of the Indian Territory.

The Osage chose the northeast section deliberately, because it was hilly and unsuitable for farming, and they reasoned that the white man would not want it. They themselves were more interested in hunting anyway, and this land was plentiful in buffalo and other game, and was good grazing land for horses. What they did not foresee was that the buffalo would soon begin to disappear, as the white man continued to settle on the wide plains and hunt them for sport and profit.

Twenty-five years after the Osage moved to Oklahoma, oil was discovered on their reservation, and the Indians suddenly found themselves very rich. Of course, their way of life was immediately affected in many ways. Soon the

Osage began riding in handsome cars instead of on spirited horses or in wagons. Because they knew nothing about cars, they hired chauffeurs to drive them. They built beautiful mansions and opened businesses. Sometimes at the back of the fine houses there would be a tipi or round lodge for the older people who preferred to live that way. Or perhaps the lodges would be used for religious ceremonies. Although by now the Osage had taken on many of the white man's ways, they had not given up their own way of worship.

Some of the older people still clung to the Indian style of dress. Many, however, wore wide-brimmed western hats decorated with a beaded band and an eagle feather. The women wore colorful shawls, usually imported, in place of blankets. Even when the Indians gave up Indian dress entirely, the men continued to wear the western hats and the women the lovely shawls. These can be seen even today. Many of the men wrap blankets around themselves in place of coats. When Indian dances, or powwows, are held, the traditional, more elaborate costumes are put on once more.

For a time it was hard for the Osage to get used to their riches. They were not familiar with handling money, especially such large amounts. All kinds of people came among them, seeking in various ways to take their money from them. Special laws had to be passed to protect the Osage from being cheated. One such law guaranteed all mineral rights to the use and benefit of the tribe and not to individual Indians. It was the Osage leaders themselves who insisted on this.

The Osage reservation officially became Osage County

in the new state of Oklahoma in 1907. At one time the government ran a school for the Indians on the reservation. All Osage children were made to go to school. Today, they go to public or private schools, colleges, and universities. There are Osage Indians living in thirty-five states and in some foreign countries. Most are employed in industry, in business, or in the professions. Traditional Indian days and ways are far behind them.

Map of Osage County, Oklahoma

CHAPTER II

Osage
Drums

In a large house surrounded by lovely gardens, a little girl was born one January day in 1925 who was to become famous around the world. She was named Elizabeth Marie Tall Chief. Her family called her Betty Marie.

The house was in Fairfax, a small town in Osage County, Oklahoma. Betty Marie's father, Alexander, was a full-blooded Osage. Her mother, Ruth Porter, was Scotch-Irish and Dutch. She had first come to Oklahoma on a vacation trip. When she met the handsome Alexander, they fell in love and were married.

Betty Marie had an older brother, Gerald, and a younger sister, Marjorie. Gerald was like his father. He loved horses and outdoor sports and he had his own pony. Marjorie was like her father, too, happy and easy-going. Betty Marie, more like her mother, was a grave and serious child.

Mrs. Tall Chief was the social leader of Fairfax, and many parties and events were held in the big house. Her home was one of culture, filled with books and lovely things. Mrs. Tall Chief wanted to give her daughters the sort of life she herself was used to. She taught them to sew and help around the house, and she started both girls on piano and dance lessons when they were young. For a treat, Betty Marie and Marjorie enjoyed going to the movies at their father's movie theater. They grew up much as any other children do in any other small town, knowing little of their Indian heritage.

Betty Marie once said that her father was the last "true Osage" in their family. He and his mother, Eliza, were Betty Marie's only link to her Osage past. She could not speak Osage; she knew only the Osage word for Tall Chief, *Ki-he-kah-stah*.

It was mostly through Grandmother Eliza, who lived with the Tall Chief family, that Betty Marie knew anything of Osage customs. Eliza would tell her stories about when she lived in a round Osage lodge and her father was a chief. When Eliza's son was born, she had carried him on her back in a cradleboard, in the traditional Osage way. Eliza explained that was the best way to carry babies — they were safe and never lonely, since they were always with their mothers. She said it had helped Betty Marie's father grow straight and stand tall, as a true "Tall Chief" should.

Sometimes Eliza would tell Osage legends from the long ago. There was a time when the animals could talk, when there were mysterious beings and strange happenings. There

An Osage community,
about 1890

were the great thunder birds that ruled the storms. There were wind and water spirits. There was magic everywhere.

Betty Marie loved these legends, and she was proud of being an Osage. She was especially proud of her great-grandfather, Chief Big Heart, the chief who had the wisdom to insist that the Indians must have the mineral rights to their land. Because of his foresight, after oil was discovered on Osage land, every Osage was receiving $15,000 a year as his share in the tribal oil money at the time Betty Marie was born. There was a painting of Chief Big Heart in the Tall Chief home. He looked as a chief should look, the young girl thought with pride.

Sometimes the Osages would get together to hold their ceremonial dances. At that time, Indian ceremonies were forbidden by the government, as was speaking the tribal language, because the government wanted the Indians to live as white people. But their customs and traditions were important to the Osages, so they continued to hold the dances in secret, far back in the hills.

Grandmother Eliza took the children with her to the dances. Betty Marie found them very exciting. Something in her responded to the beat of the drum. It had a definite rhythm, just like the beat of her heart. It was meant to be so, Eliza said, for the dancers beat upon the earth with their feet to express their emotions of anger and joy. So the drum, too, must beat, for the drum stood for the heart of the earth.

Betty Marie listened to the voices rising and falling, to the *swish-swish-swish* of gourd rattles and the sharp, clear notes of eagle bone whistles. The bells worn by the dancers added their jingle to the sounds. She realized that these dancers were people whom she saw every day in white man's dress. Now they wore beads and feathers and blankets, and their faces were strangely painted. The men wore leggings and breech cloths trimmed in beautiful ribbon work. They wore gay colored satin shirts. A scarf around their necks was held by a round shell or silver ornament. On their heads was a roach made of porcupine quills and deer hair. Usually there was an eagle feather in the roach which stood upright. Some of the leading men wore the old-style fur caps and their hair hung in braids. They wrapped themselves in red blankets.

The women wore skirts made of dark blue or black blanket material. These, too, were trimmed with ribbon work and bound at the waist with a woven yarn belt. They wore colored satin shirts, bead necklaces, beaded deer-skin leggings and moccasins, and beautiful shawls.

Betty Marie recognized one man who was a frequent visitor at the Tall Chief home. Before every dance, he announced the dance and the song that would be sung, and then he called the dancers together. There was another man who carried a whip, which he used to point at the dancers and tell them it was their turn to get up and dance.

At the end of the dance, which might last several days, there would be a feast and a "give-away." Those holding the dance would give away presents to everyone there. The fascination of the music and the beat of the drum never left Betty Marie.

When Betty Marie was a tiny child, she tried to imitate the beat of the drum on the piano. Then she began to pick out little tunes. She was three years old when it was discovered that she had perfect pitch, a rare gift. Her mother started her at once on piano lessons. She was certain that some day Betty Marie would be a concert pianist.

At four years of age, Betty Marie began to take dancing lessons. Her teacher came to the big house once a week. She taught Betty Marie to stand on her toes, to jump, leap, and spin about. As young as she was, she loved to dance. Betty Marie's mother, however, encouraged her musical talents more than her dancing, and piano practice always had to come first.

When she was five, she danced in a recital wearing a red, white, and blue dress and waving an American flag. She

Beginning to dance

whirled around the stage to the music of "The Stars and Stripes Forever." The beautiful child was a sensation.

Marjorie was now learning to dance, too, and the two girls began to perform in recitals together. With piano, dancing, and school, their days were very full. There was never much time for play. Mrs. Tall Chief did not believe that children should be idle.

When Betty Marie was eight, the Tall Chief family moved to Los Angeles. Mrs. Tall Chief felt that her daughters had grown beyond their small-town piano and dance teachers. She wanted them to have the very best, for both were talented. Alex Tall Chief was happy to move to California too, he said, because in its sunny climate he could play golf all year long. If his family were happy, it was all right with him.

A new house was found in Beverly Hills, a suburb outside of Los Angeles. Going to a new school was hard to get used to, at first. The other children laughed at the name Tall Chief. They would make "Indian war whoops" and ask questions about Indians that the children could not answer. They wondered why the girls did not wear feathers and paint their faces, or if their father had taken any scalps. But gradually, things calmed down and there was no more excitement over their being Indians. Life went on as before, except that there was even more piano and dance practice and even less time for play.

The two girls were enrolled with a fine teacher, Ernest Belcher. When he first saw them dance, he was horrified. He asked them to show him the five basic ballet positions and they did not know what they were. When Betty Marie was asked to dance, she twirled and turned on her toes, just as she had done in Fairfax. Mr. Belcher demanded that she stop. He made her remove her ballet slippers and looked carefully at her toes. "No child should dance on her toes before she is eight," he said. "It is a miracle that your feet are not badly damaged or that you are not permanently crippled."

Mr. Belcher agreed to teach the girls, but only on the condition that they join a beginner's class. They would have to unlearn everything they had learned. Day after day, the sisters practiced. They trained their muscles to be strong and flexible. They spent long hours at the *barre,* doing all sorts of exercises, over and over. There were so many rules to remember — and there was never any dancing, just practice.

Marjorie found it tiresome, but Betty Marie was intense about her dancing. Always, she tried for perfection. She even persuaded her father to put a *barre* in the house so that she could exercise at home.

As before, however, Mrs. Tall Chief was more concerned to have Betty Marie progress with her music. She wanted her to have the best instruction available, so Betty Marie enrolled in the Los Angeles Conservatory of Music. Here, too, she tried for perfection. She practiced twice a day, working hard, more for her mother than because she herself wanted to.

One day, when Mr. Belcher finally felt the two girls were ready, he let Betty Marie and Marjorie take part in a school program. They were to dance an Indian number. Betty Marie was indignant. It wasn't really Indian, she said. She and Marjorie wore Indian costumes, but they jumped and leaped around the stage as no Indian dancer

ever did. Indian women danced only with stately movements, and they were not supposed to do the stamping,
prancing steps of the men. And no Indian man ever leaped
or twirled in such fashion — even the most warlike.

Also, the drum beat of the music didn't sound Indian,
Betty Marie knew. For some reason, white people were
never able to catch the Indian beat. Their drum sounds
were stilted and their dancing looked the same way. How
easy it was to tell the white from the Indian dancer, to
hear the difference in the sound of the drum.

Marjorie was happy, though. She got to dance with a
knife in her hand and she brandished it with glee. In one
part, she even held it in her mouth! This was ever so much
better than practicing.

After this recital came a wonderful chance to be part of
the ballet of the Los Angeles Civic Opera Company. It
was only in the line, of course, but Mr. Belcher selected
only his best pupils for this honor. To Betty Marie, standing at the back of the vast stage waiting for the cue, the
moment was almost overpowering. She was so often torn
between her music and her dancing. It seemed as though
she were being pulled or pushed in two different directions,
and she was not sure which way to go. This first appearance on a real stage did much to convince Betty Marie
that she really wanted to dance. Her mother, however, was
very sure. Betty Marie was to be the musician and Marjorie
the dancer. That was the way it would be.

On her twelfth birthday, Betty Marie took part in a
piano and dance recital. She played the piano in the first
half of the recital, as perfect in her numbers as she could
be. As she played, for the first time she saw her future as

her mother saw it for her. Perhaps she would be a concert pianist, captivating an audience with her fine playing and bowing to their applause. Maybe her mother was right.

Then came the second half when she danced, light as a feather, in a gossamer yellow ballerina dress. Like Eliza in "My Fair Lady," she could have danced all night. Her heart told her that nothing else could ever take the place of dancing. But how to make her mother understand!

Her mother, watching, perhaps realized too that Betty Marie was meant to be a dancer. She had not wanted ballet to come first with her, but she sensed that it did. Still, she would not put aside her dream just yet. Betty Marie was young and many things could happen.

After a piano-ballet recital

CHAPTER III

The Flutter of Wings

Betty Marie was fourteen when she entered high school. She was liked by her classmates and they wanted to be friendly, but Betty Marie spent her entire free time in practice and study. Her school friends could not understand why she had no time for them. They thought her far too serious. Now and again Betty Marie thought wistfully of the good times she was missing. But always she stifled these thoughts and passed up the fun that beckoned.

As soon as she got up in the morning, she practiced her dancing lessons and exercises. Then she practiced on the piano before leaving for school. She practiced again when she came home until she and Marjorie left for their ballet class at five o'clock. After dinner, there were school studies to prepare for the next day.

The ballet class lasted two hours. For Betty Marie the time was short. The ballet class was the one part of her whole day that had great meaning.

The sisters were now being taught by the famous Madame Nijinska, sister of the great Russian dancer, Nijinsky. Madame Nijinska was one of the finest of teachers. She was a choreographer, or designer of ballets, as well.

Mr. Belcher had arranged an audition with Nijinska. He felt that the girls had gone far beyond what he could teach them. Nijinska was impressed and agreed to teach them if they would work hard.

Why did everyone stress that she had to work hard, Betty Marie wondered. She had never done anything else in her whole life. All of her childhood had been study and practice. She had grown up dedicated to a pattern of work. Of course she would work hard!

To Betty Marie, Nijinska was a goddess more than she was a teacher. She told stories about the glories of the Russian Ballet and of the marvelous Pavlova, its star of stars. Pavlova was someone who would never come again.

Whatever Nijinska said, Betty Marie obeyed without question. She looked up to her as a being from another world. Nijinska's smile made everything right. Her slightest frown caused Betty Marie's spirits to fall and the world to turn dark.

In her turn, Nijinska watched Betty Marie closely. She corrected over and over. No error, no matter how slight, was overlooked. It must be worked upon until it was done away with.

When touring ballet companies came to Los Angeles, Nijinska took her little flock to the performance. She impressed upon them that they must know every ballet by heart. She pointed out the various movements and criticized the dancers' faults or praised them.

"Ballet dancing must be felt with the heart," she told her students. "It must be understood with the head. The head commands what will be done, but the heart gives life to the doing. A dancer without heart is not a dancer but a puppet." She would emphasize this point often, for Nijinska would have no puppets.

More than the others, Betty Marie understood what Nijinska meant when she said, "Let the music speak to you." Her own music studies had developed in her a sympathy for melody, although this was not yet expressed in her dancing.

To her, Nijinska spoke directly. "Let the music move you," she would say. "Now you dance like one who is perfectly trained. You are a textbook dancer. This step you do because it is the way it must be done. And this step, and this step. You are so precise, my little one. Now you must strive to blend preciseness with emotion. Each perfect step must be part of each graceful movement. You must forget to be aware of the perfect way to do. I sense when you dance that you are thinking, not feeling."

When the ballets were over, Nijinska often took her students backstage. Things will look very differently than they do from the front seats, she would say. There was none of the serenity and beauty of the stage settings. The dancers scurried around and there was noise and confusion as the sets were dismantled and new ones put up for the next performance. With their strongly made-up faces, how different the dancers looked, too.

Nijinska always brought Betty Marie forward and the principals were friendly and kind. They found her great dark eyes appealing, and they knew that she was a serious, sensitive person. They encouraged her to keep on with her studies, for they had heard she was very good.

In time, Nijinska arranged for Betty Marie to take additional studies with David Lichine, a choreographer and dancer who had danced with Pavlova. His wife, Tatiana Riabouchinska, had begun her dancing career as a "baby ballerina" with the famed Ballet Russe de Monte Carlo.

Lichine, too, was a strict teacher. He demanded the best from his pupils and he pushed Betty Marie to her utmost. She strained to do what was expected of her, reaching up to higher and higher standards. She was not discouraged by hard work. It only urged her on. Mrs. Tall Chief, however, still cherished her dream that Betty Marie would one day turn away from dancing and go on with her music.

Betty Marie was fifteen and a sophomore in high school when she got her first big opportunity. She was to dance a solo part in Nijinska's ballet, *Chopin Concerto,* based on Chopin's Piano Concerto in E Minor. It would be performed in the Hollywood Bowl. Marjorie also had a part. Betty Marie was beside herself with joy and anticipation. She practiced as she had never practiced before, throwing herself into her role with all the intensity of her nature.

When the big night came, she was flawless in all of her movements. It was a beautiful night, calm and clear. Overhead, the many stars were as bright as those in Betty Marie's eyes. In the bowl thousands of people waited, but she scarcely saw them. She could only think that she must justify Nijinska's faith in her. If Nijinska would say "well done," she would ask no more.

The music started and for a time all went well. Then, as the other dancers twirled and swirled around her, Betty Marie slipped and almost fell. For one horrible moment she wanted to die, but she went on as though nothing had happened. Outwardly her poise was unshaken, and the slip was barely noticed. But to the sensitive, high-strung girl, it was an agony. Inwardly, she sobbed with embarrassment. When at last the ballet was over, she rushed offstage and into Nijinska's arms with tears flowing. But she found herself comforted instead of scolded.

"The world has not ended," Nijinska soothed. "Much worse things have happened to some of the most important dancers. There was Irina Baranova, dancing at a command performance. She made a high leap and landed on her head! Another almost lost her costume when the straps broke in the middle of a pirouette.

"It is all part of dancing," Nijinska continued. "One day you will look back at this and laugh. It is not important that you slipped. What is important is that you must rise above it." She kissed Betty Marie and said she was pleased with her.

In the papers, the next day, the critics spoke nicely of Betty Marie. Not one mentioned the mishap, and all predicted that she would be heard from in the future. The pain of that moment lingered for a long time, however. Now it is recalled with laughter, as Nijinska had said it would be — but with a fleeting sigh, too. How young she had been when that happened, and how easily wounded!

The following year there was a new teacher at Madame Nijinska's school. Mia Slavenska, who came from Yugoslavia, had danced with the Ballet Russe. When the Ballet Russe came to Los Angeles, she arranged for Serge Denham, the manager, to see Betty Marie dance.

At first he watched her classroom work. Then she danced for him in private. Mr. Denham showed no great enthusiasm. He saw hundreds of aspiring young dancers in a year, all good, but few with unusual promise. He did hold out the thought that Betty Marie could find a place with his company. It would be a way of continuing training, he said. If she were serious about her dancing, such training was essential. Many young dancers started out with high hope but gave up in the face of the hardships.

If Betty Marie joined the company, she would have to pay for her training and for her living and traveling expenses. But she would be gaining experience, and if all went well, she might become a regular member of the company.

Betty Marie was eager to go, but her mother refused to allow it. She agreed that her daughter must have talent or the offer would not have been made. She agreed that talent should be developed. But Betty Marie was too young to be on her own away from home. She must finish high school and get her diploma. Then they would talk about a career.

So Betty Marie remained at home and graduated from high school. In her final years she relaxed her strenuous schedule somewhat and allowed more time for dates and parties and school affairs. It was planned that she would attend the University of California, though she was not at all sure she wanted to go.

That summer, she found work as an extra in the *corps de ballet,* or group of background dancers, in the movie *Presenting Lily Mars.* Judy Garland was the star. Alexander Tall Chief laughed at the news. "My daughter is the first Osage ever to earn her living," he chuckled. He was proud of her, though.

The summer was happy but also disturbing. It was 1942. The United States was caught up in the anxieties of World War II. Every day friends left to join the fighting ranks or to work for the war effort. Work on the movie came to an end. Madame Nijinska and Mia Slavenska went back to the Ballet Russe. David Lichine signed with a rival company and his wife went with him.

Suddenly, Betty Marie found herself without everything and everybody familiar. But Tatiana Lichine had a suggestion. "Why don't you come to New York and finally try out for the Ballet Russe? With all of us there to look after you, your mother can't object."

Surprisingly, Mrs. Tall Chief agreed. Perhaps she reasoned that Betty Marie would be gone only a short time before entering college. A holiday would do her good. She hadn't had much fun in life.

Betty Marie could hardly believe that her mother was letting her go. On her last day at home, she gently closed the lid of her piano. It was like saying good-bye to an old friend. But she felt it was a final good-bye. She was sorry for her mother's sake. At the same time it was a relief to know that she could give herself over to ballet entirely.

In New York, she stayed with the Lichines until she could find a place for herself. On the first day, she lost no time in finding her way to Mr. Denham's offices, excitedly looking forward to telling him that she had come to begin training.

Her spirits were dashed when she was coldly turned away with a curt "He is too busy to see you." There was no encouragement given for her return. It was as though a door she thought was open had slammed in her face.

Tatiana would not allow her to stay at home and mope. That afternoon she took Betty Marie to the studio to watch the *corps* girls at practice. She was introduced to one of the girls named Helen Kramer, a warm, friendly person. They liked each other at once and became good friends.

Every afternoon there were get-togethers after rehearsal and Betty Marie became acquainted with other members of the company. She was welcomed by Madame Nijinska and Mia Slavenska, and through them she met Nathalie Krassovska, one of the great stars of the Ballet Russe. The glamorous and romantic Danilova also danced with the company.

Could she ever find a place with such famous ones as this, she wondered. Would she, an American dancer, have any chance at all? The Ballet Russe was a Russian company and all of the dancers were Russian or French, she thought, unaware that some of the names with a little change were basically American. Alicia Markova was really Alice Marks and Helen Kramer was to become Elena Kramarr. As the days went by without seeing Mr. Denham she grew even more. discouraged.

The company was soon to go on tour to Canada. Betty Marie knew that she would have to return home if she didn't have work or a definite plan very soon. Without much hope, she continued to make daily trips to Mr. Denham's office, but the answer was always the same. Finally, after a futile week, she was told to report for an audition with the company's director, Jean Yazvinsky.

At the audition, girl after girl was called up, watched with a stony face, and dismissed. Betty Marie waited until the last girl was called, but she was ignored. She was given no chance for a tryout.

Her disappointment was almost unbearable when she told the Lichines what had happened. Then she had to admit that it might have been because she had no practice clothes with her. They had been sent from California but had not arrived. Because she was in street clothes, Yaz-vinsky probably did not realize that she was there for a tryout.

"Now I will have to go home," Betty Marie told her friends. Her disappointment was even keener because she could have passed the tryout with flying colors. She knew how to do everything the director had asked for, and very well. Everyone said that her *fouettés,* which are high, whip-ping kicks, were remarkable, and her *en pointe,* or toe danc-ing, was excellent.

Tatiana refused to listen to her talk of going home. Betty Marie must stay a few more weeks. She should enroll at the School of American Ballet. Even established ballerinas continued to study and practice there and she would be using her time to good advantage.

George Balanchine was the director of the school. Betty Marie was to hear much about him. Everyone said he was a genius. His career had been a stormy one, for he had to earn his own way from the time he was a child. He had worked in a bank, as apprentice to a saddlemaker, and as pianist in a movie house. When he was twenty and still living in Russia, he formed his own ballet touring com-pany. Danilova was a member of that company and it was he who brought her to greatness. They had married, then they had parted and he had married another ballerina, Vera Zorina.

Balanchine is a creator, Betty Marie was told. He molds people to the peak of perfection — then he must go on to create another star. Little did Betty Marie know the impact this man was to have on her own life.

One night, while dining with the Lichines at the Russian

Tea Room, Tatiana pointed to a nearby table. George Balanchine was there with a group of friends. One of them was Germain Sevastianov, the manager of Ballet Theatre.

At first glance, Balanchine was a disappointment to Betty Marie. He was a small man, not at all outstanding in in appearance. I would never notice him in a crowd, Betty Marie thought. Nevertheless, she was thrilled when Balanchine and his friends moved over to the Lichines' table. The talk was all in Russian, so she could not take part in it, but she could not help but notice that Balanchine was studying her carefully. It was noticeable, too, that Sevastianov was asking questions about her.

Later, David Lichine said that Sevastianov was very much interested in her and suggested that she try out for Ballet Theatre. The company had started only three years before, but it was on the way up. New Yorkers were proud to have an American ballet and the Ballet Theatre promised to be a rival to the more established Ballet Russe.

Since the company had so many American dancers, Betty Marie resolved to ask for a tryout. She was about to do so when she was suddenly called to Mr. Denham's office and told that she would join the Canadian tour. Because of wartime restrictions, many of the Russian dancers were unable to cross the border into Canada, so the Ballet was short of girls. There would be no such difficulty with Betty Marie.

Again the promise was held out to her that if she did well and learned quickly, she would become a member of the company when the tour ended. With them, it's an "if," Betty Marie thought. Doing well and learning quickly are up to me.

How joyfully she wrote home that night. All her dreams would come true, she was sure. She said to her mother that she was unhappy to go against her wishes, but she knew that she would never appear as a pianist. Nor would she go to college. Her true love was ballet. She must follow that love wherever it led. She had made the choice.

CHAPTER IV

First
Flight

It wasn't long before Betty Marie realized that she was a war-time replacement only. She was needed for the tour, but perhaps it would be decided that she was not needed afterwards. She would have to make an impression and convince them that she had ability.

Before the company opened in Ottawa, there were hours and hours of rehearsals. Each day was a round of rehearsals and fittings. Quick meals were snatched on the run. There were only brief rest times. It was exhausting, but the excitement kept her going.

The road company was so much smaller in size that everyone had to learn a number of parts, more than they usually would. And there was less time to learn them. Betty Marie's quick memory made it possible for her to fill in many times where the other dancers could not.

One night, just before curtain time, she was told that she would have a small part in *Gaîté Parisienne*. Danilova was the star. This was a real break for her. She had to do a series of *fouettés* while on her toes. She always did them well, but never so well as she did them that night. The audience clapped loudly and the principal dancers praised her. From then on, she was given other good parts that would not otherwise have been assigned to her. She never

Snow Maiden, *Ballet Russe*

knew until almost the last moment what she would dance. Sometimes her part was changed even after she was all dressed and ready.

In Montreal, the company presented a benefit performance for the war effort. The Governor General of Canada and his wife, Princess Alice, would attend. A few days beforehand, Betty Marie was told that she would have a solo role, as Spring in the ballet, *Snow Maiden*. This important role had first been danced by Danilova. For an unknown to follow in the steps of this great ballerina was an honor and challenge. Never in her wildest dreams had Betty Marie hoped for this.

Danilova was her idol of idols. She wanted to become just like the graceful, dynamic star whom people flocked to see. All of her heart and all of her talent went into her performance. She seemed to hear Nijinska saying, "Let the music speak!" She let herself be swept along by it, and with all of her being she reached out to her audience and carried them with her. Her dancing was pure poetry, pure rapture.

That night, praise was heaped on her. Backstage callers complimented her lavishly. One of them was Princess Alice, who spoke with admiration about her lyrical dancing. "You must have worked very hard to do so well," Princess Alice said. She predicted that Betty Marie would become one of the great names in ballet. The newspaper reviews echoed the same thought the next day.

All of this was sweet to hear. Betty Marie's happiness was spoiled by only one harsh note. That was now an air of hostility towards her among the *corps* girls. They made her feel unwelcome, like an outsider.

Betty Marie knew that some of the girls thought her

standoffish. She was naturally reserved and had never had Marjorie's outgoing personality. She had studied and practiced so much by herself that she was not at ease with people. Though she could respond to friendliness and wanted to be friendly, it was hard for her to make friends at once.

The new attitude on the part of the *corps* girls was an active jealousy. They resented the fact that Betty Marie was given so many good parts. They said spitefully that this was because she was a pupil of Madame Nijinska's. There were other cutting remarks, all meant for her to hear. "Her father is a millionaire so she can ride in pullman cars while we have to go by coach," they said. They called her a "wooden Indian" and "Princess Iceberg."

Betty Marie's family had always traveled in pullman cars, so she did so as a matter of course. She had never been with a road company before and did not know it was only the principals who did so. It did not occur to her that this would set her apart from the other girls, or that they would think she thought herself too good to ride with them.

From then on, she went by coach with the rest. But the mean remarks continued. They hurt so much that she withdrew within herself and stayed pretty much alone. She was a member of the *corps* girls, but not "one of the girls."

Now she worked harder than ever. She spent what time she could watching the ballerinas practice and trying to follow their movements. This, too, aroused comment from the girls. "Trying to get in good," they sniffed. "She wants to be noticed."

The Canadian tour was a lonely and depressing experi-

ence. If it were not for her good friend Helen Kramer, it
would have been nearly unbearable. Betty Marie suffered
from the extreme cold weather and from the constant travel.
The mean remarks stung like wasps. They added to her
tiredness and discouragement. She tried to think only of
the pleasant things that took place, although the meanness
rankled. She grew pale and sad-looking. She said to Helen
that she looked like a picked chicken. She spent much of
her time resting and trying to stay well.

At last she learned to steel herself against sullen looks
and cold manners. When some of the girls complained to
the dance director that she was given parts and they were
not, she brushed this aside. She was more concerned over
what she heard him reply. "When we get back to New York
she won't have those special parts anymore," he said.
"She'll be right back in line with the rest of you."

Betty Marie wondered if she would be able to get ahead
in New York after all. Or rather, if she could get ahead
with Ballet Russe. Again she considered joining Ballet
Theatre. Her mother wrote that she was expected to return
home after the Canadian tour. This, too, she brushed aside.
She did not think at all of return — only of going ahead.

Back in New York, Betty Marie once more prepared to
call upon Germain Sevastianov of the Ballet Theatre. Once
more she was prevented from doing so. Mr. Denham sum-
moned her to his office. He had been given many good
reports about Betty Marie. Everyone said she had a glowing
future. So, he would give her a year's contract as a paid
member of Ballet Russe. There would be important roles
for her, but not at first. She might have to wait a long time
for that to happen. Always, she must work very hard. There

would be disappointments and frustrations and constant practice.

"If you can't stand up to it all, then you must decide to leave now," Mr. Denham said flatly. "You have got to have what it takes to be a dancer. I think you do."

Betty Marie answered yes at once. Practice she was not afraid of; that she had always done. Hard work she was not afraid of. She had always worked hard. Disappointment she could learn to accept. She would stay with Ballet Russe and hang on, come what may. All that mattered was that she would be dancing. The chance would come to prove herself. She could wait for as long as it took. She would not stay in the *corps* forever.

The New York season began almost at once. On opening night, Betty Marie arrived early. The great stage was ready. Soon the musicians would tune their instruments. The electricians would test their lights. The giant theater would come to life.

In the dressing room, excitement was high. Betty Marie expected to dance the cancan in *Gaîté Parisienne* with a group of *corps* girls. It was a spirited number and she always enjoyed it. She hurried to get ready, pulling on her long hose and slipping her costume with its flouncy skirts over her head. Makeup was put on carefully. A large flower was fastened in the sleek hair. A velvet ribbon was fastened around her throat.

The dressing room was crowded and noisy so she waited in the wings. It was nearly time for the audience to start arriving. Suddenly, a hand was placed on her shoulder and she was given a quick shove.

"Hurry, get out of that costume," she heard the dance

director say. "You are going to dance a solo. The soloist who performs the role has not arrived. She cannot be waited for."

Unfastening her costume as she went, Betty Marie ran back to the dressing room. The wardrobe mistress had her new costume ready for her. Her makeup had to be changed. In only a few moments she was ready and about to leave for the wings. She intended to go over her steps.

Just then the soloist dashed in. There was scarcely time for her to get into the costume which Betty Marie quickly slipped off. She smiled as she gave it to the dancer, but she wanted to cry.

There was a titter among the *corps* girls. They were laughing at her. One girl said, "Miss High and Mighty didn't make it this time." Betty Marie remained silent. Only her great dark eyes flashed anger. She would be a good trouper and let no one see how badly she felt. She would not give the girls the satisfaction of letting their jabs upset her.

Quickly she became a cancan dancer again. She danced with a smile on her face, lifting her long tapering legs in perfect *fouettés*. She knew she did them better than anyone else. It gave her a bitter-sweet feeling to see the envious looks of the other dancers. They know it too, she thought. Let them laugh at me if they want to.

As she danced off into the wings, the dance director was waiting. With him was the wardrobe mistress holding out a new costume. The director's face was scarlet. This costume was for another ensemble. Someone had not shown up and Betty Marie had to fill in. Her new dress was barely fastened when she was back on stage.

That night there was a party after the ballet. "You have earned the right to better roles," Mia Slavenska said. "You will have them. But Mr. Denham wants you to have a new name — a Russian one."

Betty Marie refused. She did not want a different name. She wanted to dance as herself. But Mia said that the name Betty Marie was a childish one. It was not the name for someone who will be a great star.

Someone suggested the name of Tallchieva. What could be more Russian than that?

To this, Betty Marie also said no. "I will not change my last name," she said. "It's a good American name. I'm proud of it. I'm not a Russian."

No amount of argument could persuade her. Even Mr. Denham tried to win her over. "I'll change my first name," she finally gave in. "You can call me Maria. But Tall Chief must stay as it is. You can spell it as one word, if you want to." So it was decided. Maria Tallchief she would be. Maria Tallchief, the Osage dancer. Maria Tallchief, who would go a long way.

When she wrote home to her family, Maria said that it seemed like a miracle. But then, to dance was a miracle. She spoke no word of the mean things that had taken place. She talked only of the promise that lay ahead. When she put aside the name Betty Marie, she also put aside childish feelings. As Maria, she had become a woman.

She had tried out her wings and they had carried her on her first flight. She was eager, now, to fly to new heights.

CHAPTER V

The Wings
Grow Strong

Six months after Maria first came to New York, she had a small part in *Rodeo*. This was a new, modern ballet choreographed by Agnes de Mille. It met with tremendous success, and it was a small success for Maria. But she was not enjoying herself. She was continually depressed, did not eat well, and grew steadily thinner. It was like a sickness, but she was not sick except in spirit.

Shortly before taking the *Rodeo* part, the Ballet Russe had announced that Madame Nijinska's *Chopin Concerto* would be included in the list of presentations. The names of the cast were posted, but Maria's name was not among them. She tried to tell herself she had been an amateur when she danced the ballet. She was still no more than a small-part dancer. She could hardly expect to be included.

Yet, she longed to dance the *Concerto* with all of her being. Her experience in the Hollywood Bowl came back to haunt her. To dance the ballet well would be to wipe out that early mishap. Surely she could have been given a tiny part! She wanted to dance the *Concerto* so badly that she could think of little else.

Day after day she watched Krassovska rehearse the same role that she had once danced. The movements had been changed somewhat. She studied as she watched so that they became familiar to her. She could have filled in for any of the soloists if an emergency arose, so well did she study all their parts.

When *Chopin Concerto* opened in the Metropolitan Opera House, Maria watched from the wings. She saw herself in every turn, in every graceful position. Her imagining was so vivid it was almost real. But it wasn't real, she was forced to admit. She was only standing on the sidelines.

The program was a great triumph. Danilova, the prima ballerina, received ovation after ovation. Krassovska, too, was applauded enthusiastically. Maria was delighted for her beloved Danilova, for her friend Krassovska, and for Madame Nijinska. But her delight was edged with despair. When was the promised time coming when she would be a great star? Where were the important roles she had been promised? She worked so hard, tried so hard, did everything that was asked of her — and stayed where she was.

In spite of her worries, Maria continued to perfect and polish her dancing. She practiced by herself for hours on end. She paid for extra lessons with her own money. She grew more wan and thin, and she was more than ever driven to succeed.

That fall, the company went on tour. Maria danced in Los Angeles for the first time since she had left home. She did not have a solo part, however, but was still one of the *corps* girls. It was good to see her family again. Marjorie was doing well with her dancing and was certain to find a future in ballet. Mrs. Tall Chief worried about Maria. She was troubled to see her looking so poorly. "You should come home and rest," she urged. "You should stay here and dance. Maybe you should even give up ballet. It is too hard on you."

The ballet returned to New York for a Christmas Day opening. Maria worked for an hour by herself. Then, while she was exercising at the *barre,* the dance director approached her. He said that it was possible she would dance in the *Concerto* the following night. Krassovska was ill and Maria would be allowed to dance that role. She was to stay after the performance and practice the changes.

Maria almost collapsed with joy. It was as though a magic wand had been waved and lifted her up to the clouds. The news spread quickly through the cast and many warm wishes were spoken for good luck. Some of the girls who had been the most unfriendly had left the company and there were better feelings toward Maria. It was admitted that she had been given parts because she deserved them. Maria had something that the rest did not — an inner spark and more than the usual amount of skill.

That night Maria was ready long before curtain time. Then came a message. Danilova wished to see her. Maria hurried to her dressing room and found Mr. Denham there, also. He looked troubled.

As Maria waited with a sinking heart, the two talked in Russian. Somehow, she knew what was being said. She clasped her hands tightly together, afraid for what she would hear.

"Danilova does not think you are ready for the *Concerto,*" Mr. Denham said. "She says you have had no proper rehearsal. She says that you cannot master this difficult role in only a day's time."

Maria pleaded that she could. She knew all of the movements and the music. It was time for the curtain call, so there the matter was left.

The following night, Maria was at the theater early. Her friends clustered around her, eager to help with her hair, her costume, her makeup, or just to be near her in this wonderful hour. When she was ready, she stood in her usual place in the wings.

Then Mr. Denham touched her on the shoulder. She turned, her face shining with happiness. Mr. Denham could not look at her. "You will not be needed," he said shortly, and walked away.

Crushed, Maria went back to the dressing room. The *corps* girls were shocked at her stricken face. No one said a word as she blindly took off her costume and left the room. She stumbled home to sit alone in darkness.

Nothing so terrible had ever happened to her before. "Why? why?" she asked herself over and over. There had to be a reason. But the reason would not come. Only the hurt mounted and mounted.

For the next few days, rumors spread like wildfire. Maria was the talk of the ballet world. There were times when she wanted to run away and hide. But she had an inner toughness, an inner strength, that carried her through. She refused to be defeated by what had taken place. She stayed calm and would not discuss what had happened or what was said.

At last Danilova spoke to her. "Don't hate me," she said. "There just wasn't enough time for you to dance *Concerto*. If you had not done well, your whole career would have been set back. Some day you will dance the *Concerto* and you will be wonderful."

Danilova had a small part for Maria in *Le Beau Danube* and urged her to take it. So Maria swallowed the lump in her throat and began rehearsing. She tried to be grateful for Danilova's attention. She would keep on doing her best.

The winter was a rugged one. One after another, the dancers became ill. Maria, too, caught a cold and was unable to shake it. She was given a solo part in *Schéhérazade,* but her spirits remained low and her health poor. Mrs. Tall Chief again wrote for her to come home. She sensed in Maria's letters that she wasn't well. Marjorie was studying with Madame Nijinska and Maria could study with her.

Maria hung on doggedly. She would not let go. She went on tour with the company in April, even though she was very ill. Her mother wrote again that Marjorie was dancing with the Los Angeles Light Opera Company. Maria must come home. A place would be found for her with the same company.

Again Maria refused. She had a contract with Ballet Russe and would not break it. Once she fainted at a private party. Her friends were alarmed over her health, and she begged them not to let her mother know. She continued to practice and dance, even when she should not have done so.

Then came a never-to-be-forgotten day. May 1, 1943! The day of the big chance, at last!

Krassovska injured her foot and Maria was told that she would take her place in the matinee performance of *Concerto*. She tried to stand quietly while she was being fitted for her costume. But the words "I will show them" kept singing through her head. "I will show them. I will SHOW THEM." She wanted to leap around the room.

When the cue came, she did leap onstage and swirled

Theme and Variations

Schéhérazade

The Firebird

Swan Lake

into the steps as if she were another being. She was part of the music, dancing as if in a dream. She was a new and different Maria, radiant, following her heart in the joy of dancing.

She finished to thunderous applause. Even Danilova stood aside as she took her bows. She had proven that she was a dancer — a great dancer. She was the only girl in the company with the promise of becoming a prima ballerina. There was no higher place to go.

All of the principals were elated. They had witnessed the birth of a star. Mr. Denham, in his quiet way, complimented her, too. She would dance the Krassovska role until the foot had recovered. But even when Krassovska returned, Maria continued to dance the role although it was Krassovska's name that appeared in the program. She did not mind. It was not the glory but the doing that mattered.

When Ballet Russe opened its summer season, Krassovska decided to go to Europe. Maria now had the *Concerto* role for good. So far, she had danced it only on tour. Now she would debut in the ballet in New York City. She was only eighteen years old! The world was very good.

Mr. Denham understood the happiness that shone from her eyes. He had been concerned over her sunken cheeks and her pale face. But he knew that happiness was a great healer. Maria's health began to improve almost at once with the *Concerto* assignment.

The New York debut was outstanding. There was no question now of her stature as a dancer. Tears stood in her eyes as she saw the audience rise and heard their shouts and applause. Many bouquets of flowers were brought to the stage. One of them touched her deeply. It was a huge bouquet of roses from the corps girls.

Even though she continued to dance as a *corps* girl and in small parts, she was the star of *Concerto*. People flocked to the theater when the ballet was announced. Newspaper reporters demanded to interview her. They spoke of her as the beautiful dancing Osage, the Osage Indian Princess. They wanted stories about her life in a tipi and how she rode a pony across the plains. Could she shoot a bow and arrow, they wanted to know, and did her father wear a feather headdress?

Maria protested there were no stories of that kind to tell. She had never lived in a tipi. Her people did not live in Indian fashion. She was not a princess. Indians did not have royal titles. There was nothing romantic about her life. Her father was an expert golfer. He had never worn eagle feathers. Besides, she wanted to rise in her profession as a dancer, not because she was an Osage Indian.

For Maria, life would never again be the same. When the season was at an end, Mr. Denham lost no time in offering her a new two-year contract. In spite of Maria's pleas, Mrs. Tall Chief would not let her sign it. She was critical of the company for making Maria wait so long for the *Concerto* part. She was bothered, too, because she heard that Krassovska was coming back to the company. The controversial George Balanchine was to be the new choreographer and dance director, and that would mean more changes and uncertainties.

"You should not tie yourself down," Mrs. Tall Chief advised. "With Krassovska back, you will have fewer chances. Balanchine will have his own favorites. You may find yourself pushed aside."

Mr. Denham was very annoyed. In the end, he had to agree that Maria could return without a contract. That was the only way he could get her. He did say that he could not give her important roles unless he knew that she would stay with the company. It was not long before Maria realized her mother was right. Krassovska did come back. Quite a few new names were listed in the cast. One, who had come with Balanchine, was immediately featured, even though Maria was the better dancer. Mr. Denham showed his annoyance in other ways.

When Madame Nijinska returned to the company, Maria was given a part in one of her ballets. *Etude* was first performed in Cleveland while the company was on tour. Maria did not care for it and did not enjoy dancing it. The audiences did not care for it either.

To make matters worse, the company was getting very poor press notices. It was constantly compared unfavorably with Ballet Theatre. The rival company was arousing interest through new and dramatic presentations. Because these broke with classical tradition, they were of interest to American tastes. The many American dancers with the company also found favor.

When Maria saw some of the Ballet Theatre programs she was delighted with them. She began to think once again of applying with the company. There seemed no chance for her at all with Ballet Russe. Things did not improve until Balanchine took over active direction of the company.

CHAPTER VI

Dancing
with Balanchine

Under Balanchine, Ballet Russe was restored and revived. It could compete with Ballet Theatre and hold its own. Balanchine's great skill lay in the way he could inspire his dancers. He was patient with them, but he never let up until he had forced them into the exact effect that he wanted.

"He makes puppets of us all," some of the dancers complained. But Maria worked for him tirelessly, doing over and over what he wanted until it became a part of her. She felt herself growing, changing, taking on more depth. She became more and more the kind of dancer she had always envisioned as the ideal.

She was happy working with Balanchine. Her happiness was greater when Marjorie came to New York to dance with Ballet Theatre. The two sisters were very fond of each other, and very close. For New Yorkers, it was something new to have sisters starring with different companies. It became the fashion to go from one theater to the other on the nights when both were dancing. Maria, however, had not seen Marjorie dance since they danced together as children, nor did she in New York. Program schedules interfered.

Maria was given a part in *Ballet Imperial* created by

Balanchine. She knew the music well, but for some reason she was not at home in the part. Perhaps she tried too hard, or was too tense. She was barely mentioned by the critics.

Balanchine was not at all dismayed, and he would not let Maria be. Instead, he cast her in *Les Sylphides*. In this, she was sensational. The critics were lavish in their praise. They questioned if she could repeat a performance that was such sheer magic. Could it be that way again?

Balanchine laughed at the critics. He knew that Maria could and would go on to even greater performances. He had plans that would establish her greatness.

More and more important roles came her way, and more and more she danced in the Balanchine style. More and more, too, Maria and Balanchine were talked about and not just as artists. Balanchine paid special attention to her roles. They were seen having dinner together. Both deeply musical, they found a mutual interest in talking over the scores and how they should be interpreted.

When it was learned that Balanchine and Vera Zorina were seeking a divorce, the talk about Maria grew. Now we know it is more than professional interest, the company said. Balanchine had married, one after another, the girls he had brought to stardom.

One day he told Maria that he intended to produce *Le Baiser de la Fée* ("The Fairy's Kiss"). The ballet is based on a fairy tale written by Hans Christian Andersen called "The Ice Maiden."

Maria was overcome when he calmly said that she was to be the fairy. It was the most important part she had ever danced. The story is about a baby boy left to die in the snow. The fairy finds him and kisses him to life, but her kiss also binds him to her forever. When he is grown, he is to marry a girl of his village. At the wedding, his bride turns into the fairy, who carries him below the waters of a frozen lake. She kisses him again — a kiss in which both life and death combine.

Mia Slavenska had danced this role a few years before. What made it so difficult was that the dancer had to portray three different personalities. Maria would have to be the queenly Ice Maiden, a mysterious gypsy fortune-teller, and the young bride. At the same time, she must make it clear to the audience that she was really the fairy.

Balanchine wrote the dance expressly for Maria. He designed it to show off her fluid grace and amazing skill. He did not ask if she could do it. He simply said that she would do it. Rehearsals would start at once. With such confidence placed in her, Maria had confidence, too. If Balanchine said she could do it, he would make certain that she did. She had only to follow his direction.

The ballet was the most important presentation of the new season. The theater was packed for the performance with an audience that was frankly curious about Maria, whom they spoke of as the latest "Balanchine ballerina." They came to judge her, and they saw a performance so superior that it would never again be equalled. Onstage that night, a great new ballerina was born.

It was as if Maria were truly a fairy with fairy powers. Before their very eyes she changed from the regal Ice Maiden to a wild gypsy, to a lovely bride and back to the coldly glittering Ice Maiden again. Each part was danced with unbelievable skill.

The audience and the critics raved. The theater rang with their cheers. They would hardly let Maria leave the stage. For some time, the critics had hailed her as a ballerina, and they did so again. But the Ballet Russe had never given her this title. In the tradition of Russian ballet, it was not given lightly and never to one who had not proved herself many times. Only two dancers held the title with the company — Danilova, the *prima,* or first, ballerina, and Krassovska.

Ten days after the fairy ballet, Maria was starred in *Night Shadow,* a new Balanchine ballet. In this, she was completely different, a hard, sexy woman, a flirt, a coquette. On opening night, she was frankly nervous. Could she be convincing in this role, so unusual a one for her? Also, she was dancing for the first time with a new partner — Nicholas Magallanes. Would they be liked as a pair?

Danilova, too, had a part in *Night Shadow.* For once, she was not the attraction. It was Maria the people came to see and they loved her performance. Again she was hailed as a ballerina and still the Ballet Russe did not give her the title.

Maria did not let this bother her. Balanchine gave her more and more important roles. She was delighted that she pleased him. To her, he was the most marvelous of men. Professionally, they were right for each other. Balanchine knew just how to bring her out, to put her, like a rare jewel, in a beautiful setting. She was just what he needed to perfect his creations. He spoke of her as his diamond, and like a diamond, he polished and polished her, bringing out new facets until she was the most brilliant of all his gifts to the art of ballet.

In 1946, at the peak of his career, Balanchine shocked the company by announcing his resignation. With a former partner, he planned to form a new company called Ballet Society. With Balanchine gone, what would happen to Ballet Russe? What would happen to Maria Tallchief?

A month after his resignation, Balanchine and Maria Tallchief were married. He was twenty years older than she. Everyone thought that Maria, too, would leave the company. She did not. She was under contract until the summer of 1947 and would finish it out. To her, a contract was a promise and a promise must be kept. She did, however, plan for the time when she could join her husband.

When the company went on tour, Maria was billed as the Osage Indian Princess. It did no good to protest. This kind of publicity helped to arouse interest. On matters like this, the publicity department ruled. Thousands of people in every city came to see the fabulous Danilova and the equally fabulous Tallchief. Wherever Maria went, she was mobbed by fans. People waited in line to see her, to ask for her photograph or her autograph. She was heaped with flowers, gifts, and boxes of cookies and candy. She blossomed under all this attention, for it was exciting to be the object of so much admiration.

At the same time, Maria worried. People expected so much of her. She would have to constantly strive to live up to their expectations.

With Maria now a star of first rank, the Ballet Russe decided that she had really earned the title of ballerina — the only American ballerina in history. They tried to persuade her to remain with the company. They pointed out that Ballet Society was only just getting started. It was a small company and had small audiences. They did not want to let their prize get away from them.

Maria only shook her head. Ballet Society was her husband's company, and she wanted to be with Balanchine. Again, she had a contract, a marriage contract this time. That was more of a solemn promise than a business one.

In her final weeks with Ballet Russe, Maria colored every role she danced with the fire of her personality. She had changed very much from the rather shy, withdrawn young girl who had first come to New York. She was radiant, vibrant, a glowing ember, lighted by happiness and success. The ovations that had once belonged to Danilova were now hers. Nobody could believe that she would cast all that aside and leave the company. Surely she would change her mind.

But Maria was looking forward to going to Paris. Balanchine was there. At the end of the New York season, he had accepted the position of ballet master and choreographer at the Opera. Maria's sister Marjorie was also in France, where she and her husband George Skibine were principal dancers with the Grand Ballet du Marquis de Cuevas. They lived in the south of France.

Balanchine planned to feature Tamara Toumanova as guest prima ballerina. She was one of his discoveries and had first danced in Paris when she was a child. She was expected to be a sensation, and ballet lovers from all over Europe would come to see her.

In Paris there were some unfriendly feelings for Balanchine, who was thought too radical in his approach to traditional ballet. This hostility was strengthened with Maria's arrival. No American had danced at the Paris

Rehearsing with Balanchine

Opera in more than a hundred years. Many people felt that no American was good enough to dance there. Balanchine won't dare to put Tallchief on the Opera stage, and especially not with Toumanova, these people speculated. But Balanchine not only might, he did. He presented Maria again as the Fairy in *Le Baiser de la Fée,* for it was in this role that she was shown off most dramatically.

The Parisian audience came prepared to "boo." Instead, they reacted with awe. The newspapers said that Tallchief made magic with every step. Those that saw her talked of little else. Everyone wanted to see her. Give us Tallchief, the extraordinary American dancer, they implored.

After a short time in Paris and a visit with Marjorie, the Balanchines returned to New York. Balanchine at once insisted that Maria must return to ballet school. In spite of her triumph in Paris, he said that she had forgotten some basic techniques. So back to school Maria went. She never questioned any of Balanchine's opinions or decisions.

New Yorkers clamored to see her again, and she was soon ready to go back to work. The Ballet Society, however, was not ready for her. She could no longer be cast in anything but the finest parts. Her special skills required magnificent settings and this took a great deal of money. The Ballet Society had almost no money at all.

Still, Balanchine was able to work wonders with her. He created little gems of exquisite ballet that were designed especially for her. He had another exceptionally good dancer, too, named Tanaquil LeClercq, who was as different from Maria as night from day. Maria was proud and mysterious, while Tanaquil was sunny and gay.

To show them at their best, Balanchine made miniature

ballets for them. These were so well received that Ballet Society gained in favor. In one season, it gained public support and a permanent home in the New York City Center Theatre.

It was here that Balanchine presented *Orpheus,* a new offering. Maria was starred as Eurydice and Nicholas Magallanes as Orpheus. Tanaquil had another leading role.

The ballet was spectacular and Maria was breathtaking. She was awarded the Annual Dance Magazine Award for this performance: for "memorable lyric quality, for a discipline beautiful to see, for command and growing compassion."

After this, Maria had her first vacation in six years of dancing. She and Balanchine returned to Europe where he would choreograph and direct the company for which Marjorie and George Skibine danced. Marjorie and Skibine danced beautifully together, and their partnership was making dance history.

When the Balanchines again returned to the United States, they looked forward to a bright future. Balanchine was now being praised instead of criticized. His *Orpheus* was said to have opened a new era in dramatic ballet. Maria, too, was praised for her part in it. The Ballet Society was now firmly entrenched under a new name, the New York City Ballet Company.

Ballet lovers looked for new and bigger thrills from Balanchine and more and greater dramatic roles for Maria. But creative persons cannot create on demand. They must go at their own pace. They must follow their own inspirations and impulses. Balanchine had nothing definite in mind. He could only produce to suit himself.

Maria, too, suffered from the public's expectations. They wanted to see her in important roles and stunning productions. These had to be created for her. Until they were, she had only the same parts to dance.

For this season, Ballet Russe was strong competition. They had a number of stars that constantly drew large audiences. Because New York City Ballet had to share its quarters with the New York City Opera Company, they were further hampered by being able to play only a short season.

Because of the short season, Maria accepted an invitation to be a guest ballerina with Ballet Theatre. Her partner was the great Igor Youskevitch. She was as awed by him as when she had first met him as a child, when Madame Nijinska had taken her backstage in Los Angeles. Youskevitch had patted her on the head and called her a "grave, graceful child."

At first, she could not dance well with Youskevitch. She was too overcome by her feelings. But Youskevitch knew how to make her respond to him. He helped her to put aside her shyness and they danced together in an unforgettable partnership. They were so ravishing that audiences were completely bewitched.

Now people wondered if Balanchine could possibly find a role for Maria that could recreate the splendor that Ballet Theatre had achieved.

Balanchine, meanwhile, was making his own plans. He was creating something exactly right — a dazzling something that would stun the ballet world and leave them gasping. And Maria would shine as the most glorious of all living ballerinas. He never doubted that this would be so.

CHAPTER VII

The Miracle of the Firebird

It was on November 27, 1949, that Balanchine's great plan for Maria Tallchief became reality, in his presentation of *The Firebird*. This Fokine ballet, based on a Russian folk tale, had been performed many times. But Balanchine had created a new and far more thrilling version. He dressed it in Oriental splendor, sparing no expense to get the richness and color he wanted.

When Maria was first told that she was to be the Firebird, she gasped with shock and dismay. There was only one week to prepare for the role. That was an almost superhuman task in itself. She was frankly worried. How could she be the wonderful, exotic, supernatural creature, half-bird, half-woman? For once her courage failed. She told Balanchine that she couldn't do it.

Balanchine understood her feelings. He was always gentle with her, even when he was under strain. He said softly, "You can, you can. You know you can." And suddenly, Maria knew she could. Back into her mind drifted her grandmother Eliza's stories of long ago, of the spirit beings that once lived upon the earth. Fire was not just fire to the Osages. It was real, it had life and power. The Firebird became real to her.

There were those that thought both Balanchine and

Maria were attempting too much. Some asked Maria how she could get ready for so demanding a role in a week's time. There were just too many difficulties. There were variations that required great technical skill. To this Maria would answer that one does what one has to do, and when they must they do a little more. She really believed it.

On the night of the presentation, Maria waited in the wings. She shivered, not with cold, but with excitement. Balanchine had gone against tradition to make this interpretation distinctly his own. He had staked his reputation and the future of his company to bring this myth of the Russian steppes to a passionate portrayal. He had fought against those who protested the liberties he took with the libretto. He had clung to his certainty that he had found the ideal person to climax the whole, to make of the Firebird what it should be, a savage, fantastic, iridescent being from a timeless past. And now, everything depended on Maria.

Soon the great curtain would rise and she would dance out upon the stage. Balanchine had filled her mind with the certainty that in this role she would reach the highest point of her career. There could be no failure. She well understood the burden of responsibility that was hers.

For one solid week, Balanchine had driven his dancers almost beyond their endurance. He had driven her, hammering away as though shaping steel on a forge. Through his force and will, Balanchine had drawn her, step by step, dance by dance, to the peak that now waited her. He had brought her to the heights. Now she must go far above and beyond all that she had yet given of herself. Through his force, again, he must lift her, thrust her, release her. If she did not find that release, that soaring, she would remain in his grasp forever — perfection in chains.

Because he understood this, Balanchine came to her as she waited. He kissed her trembling hands. He told her not to be frightened, to see the colors, the lighting, to hear the beat of the music, to feel them. "They are of you and you are they, all the flame, all the color, all the heart beat," he said. "You are no longer the little high school girl who came to New York seven years ago. You are no longer the dancer of pure accomplishment. You are no longer my wife. You are yourself — Maria Tallchief. This is your moment and you must make the most of it."

Silently, they stood side by side. The cast took their places in silence. The backstage quiet was unusual. The tension was terrific.

In the theater, the huge audience hummed with talk. Tallchief is exquisite, flawless, they said, but she is more the Ice Maiden than a bird of fire. Many felt that Balanchine had made the wrong choice. As much as they loved Maria, they felt this ballet was for a Russian dancer.

Igor Stravinsky, the conductor, took his place in the orchestra pit as the stage lights went on. The curtain slowly began to rise. There was a ripple of delighted applause for the stunning set, and then an expectant hush.

In one great leap, Maria soared onto the stage. She was in awesome control of herself. She crossed and recrossed the stage in fantastic *jetés,* or leaping movements. She flew as she danced, she danced as she flew. She left the audience breathless with ecstasy. This was enchantment. Surely Maria had to be enchanted to become so forcefully this supreme artist.

In a costume of glittering sequins, arms and shoulders shining with gold dust, on her head a crest of fiery plumes, on her feet crimson slippers, she was enveloped in a sheath of flame. She danced as no human being had ever danced. She was not human. She *was* the Firebird.

At last it was over, the tumult, the bravas, the repeated curtain calls. Maria, exhausted, sat alone in her dressing room. When she was a child, she would look in the mirror on her birthday. She wanted to see if she looked any older, any taller. Now she looked intently in the glass as she had done then.

With makeup off, she saw the same face, the same large, dark eyes. She was Maria still. But this time, there was a difference. The mirror showed a new authority, a new radiance, a new expressiveness. They would mark her from this day on. She stared in the glass, seeing herself through all of the years that had brought her to this triumph. She walked again the road she had traveled to become what she now was — one of the greatest ballerinas of all time.

For the first time in its history, the New York City Ballet now played to packed houses. The reviewers of *The Firebird* all marveled at Maria's performance. Everyone in New York, it seemed, wanted to see her. The demand was so great that other performances of the ballet were scheduled. With every one the applause was thunderous.

The rival Ballet Theatre responded to Maria's greatness and invited her to join the company as guest prima ballerina. This meant that she would be given only the choicest roles, such as had been given to Danilova with Ballet Russe. There is no higher title than that of prima.

Maria as the Firebird,
with Francisco Moncion

With the close of the season, Maria joined Ballet Theatre in Chicago where the company was on tour. Ballet Theatre had some of the works of Balanchine in its repertoire but did not use them. They were not liked by audiences or dancers. Both complained they could not understand them.

With Maria, it was thought that this problem would be overcome. Maria danced each one brilliantly. Away from the sophisticated New York audiences, however, the ballets fell flat. They were still not appreciated. Maria was not the success she should have been. She was relieved when the tour ended and she could return to New York.

With the opening of the New York City Ballet's spring season, she once more danced *The Firebird*. The audience was so stunned with the beauty of the performance that for a few seconds they sat in silence. The performance had been too perfect to spoil the effect with noise. Then the applause broke forth and nearly took down the walls.

It was a deeply moving experience for Maria. The intense feeling that was aroused and her overtaxed body brought her to a state of nervous tension. She was often between tears and laughter and she badly needed rest. But Balanchine had no thought of rest for his diamond dancer. He immediately cast her in the role of the siren in *The Prodigal Son*.

For once, Balanchine miscalculated. His interpretation of the siren was not in accord with the Biblical story. The part was not right for Maria and she completely failed in it. This disaster was a sharp blow to her pride. It was not Balanchine's fault, but hers, she reasoned. She worried, too, over her prima position. With the New York City

Ballet she could maintain it only if she continued to measure up. It was not like the Ballet Russe where the prima retained her title for always.

Maria continued to be as wonderful as ever in *The Firebird*. She could not, however, keep going on the strength of a single role, no matter how outstanding. She had to excel in a number of others. There was no other ballet in which she could equal the performance of the Firebird. She grew increasingly apprehensive.

Balanchine still encouraged her, saying he would find something else. Then the company was invited to appear in London. Balanchine had to spend all of his time in preparation for this. New ballets were out of the question.

When the company arrived in London, the dancers were appalled. The stage of the Royal Opera House was far too vast. They would be lost on such a giant stage. All of their training had been on a small stage. Their ballets, too, were small in design. They were the little gems that were the specialty of Balanchine.

Good troupers all, they did their very best. But they were not well received. Maria, too, met with disappointing reception. Londoners did not care for *The Firebird* at all. It was too strange, too flamboyant, too overpowering for their tastes. Surprisingly, they liked *The Prodigal Son*.

Maria was depressed by the indifference to *The Firebird*, for she loved this role. It was so essentially hers that the coolness seemed a rejection of herself. She hoped for a warmer response to Balanchine's *Serenade*. It was more nearly in the British style. As the ballet started, however, she found herself unable to go on. Other unfortunate events were to follow.

The most tragic and shattering of all was the breakup of her marriage. Maria felt that she had failed as a woman. She forgot that throughout his life Balanchine had married and left those whom he made great. He was being true to a pattern of behavior. It was hard to apply this to herself, to accept that it could happen to her, too. Her self-blame was sad and bitter.

Even though not married, the Balanchines would continue in their professional relationship. This, too, was typical of Balanchine, who had continued to direct each of his wives in future ballets.

Maria brooded over the changed situation for some time. Marriage is important, she finally decided, and dancing is important, too. They should be taken one at a time. She began to see, now, that Balanchine had married her because of his ambitions for her, and for himself. He loved her, but more as a ballerina than as a woman. He had achieved his ambition. Now there must be a new dancer to build to stardom. When she could take this objective view, the hurt was eased a little though it could not leave her entirely.

At the time when she most needed something good to happen, it did. Maria was finally given a perfect partner. This was André Eglevsky. He was just right for Maria and for Balanchine as well. With Tallchief and Eglevsky, Balanchine now had the pair who could most outstandingly dance the *pas de deux* (a dance for two) in his ballets.

Eglevsky had danced with every major company in the world. He had danced with all of the great ballerinas. He knew just how to display his partners at their best. With Maria, he now had a partner who did this for him.

The two were incomparable. Praise for them was so great that European audiences demanded to see them. Balanchine finally agreed to another European tour. The company first appeared in Zurich, Switzerland. There, Maria danced the role of the Swan Queen in Swan Lake. The people flocked to see the beloved ballet with two exciting dancers. At the end, they knew they had seen the "performance of a lifetime." It was so described by the reviewers. Maria was called back for fifteen bows. The audience cheered and whistled in a way Swiss audiences usually did not do.

From Switzerland, the company went to Holland where the triumph was repeated. The whole tour was a continuous success. Life was looking up again.

Her spirits lifted, Maria was again in love. This, too, she needed, to restore her to herself. When the company returned to New York, she married the young charter airline pilot, Elmourza Natirboff, who had won her heart. He was as far removed from ballet as one could be, but he was fun, and charming and handsome. He was good for a woman, still young, who was putting her life together again. Maria forgot her decision that marriage and ballet should not be taken together, for she intended to continue with her career.

Balanchine, too, remarried. This time his wife was Tanaquil LeClercq. He had found his new dancer.

CHAPTER VIII

Osage Princess, Ballet Queen

For the next two years, Maria Tallchief was hailed the world over. Every appearance was a personal triumph. She danced many roles, for people just wanted to see her. What she danced made no difference. There was an outpouring of tribute from every part of the globe.

Among others, the people of Oklahoma were especially proud of their native daughter. The State Legislature, in a significant gesture, proclaimed June 29, 1953, as Maria Tallchief Day. There was no one in the state who did not know who Maria Tallchief was.

The Osages, too, were not to be outdone. They asked that Maria return to Fairfax where her parents were once again living. Special ceremonies were to be held. As in the old days, she would be given an "honor name." There would be dancing and a feast of Indian foods, the delicious Indian corn boiled with beef, and Indian "fried bread." Few can eat these foods without wanting more.

Of all the honors that came to her, Maria was most pleased by the action of the Osage Tribe. She was the more deeply touched when told that her Grandmother Eliza had chosen her name. It was Wa-Xthe-Thonba, which means "Woman of Two Standards." It meant that Maria belonged to the Osage people but she also belonged to the people of her mother as well. More than that, through this name her people were telling her that she had upheld the dignity of the Osage while winning honors in the world.

As Maria watched the dancing, memories of her childhood came flowing back to her. The dancers were far more resplendent than those she had seen with Grandmother Eliza. These were dressed in gorgeous beaded garments. Many wore eagle feather bonnets and softly tanned buckskins. They were handsome, indeed. But the drum beat was the same, the voices, high and shrill, were the same, and the spirit of "Indian-ness," or One-ness, was the same.

One song was sung especially for Maria. This, too, was a custom of the old days when heroes and leaders were honored with songs composed for them and sung for no one else.

For the first time in her life, Maria took part in an Indian feast, ate Indian food, and felt like a true Osage. She wished that she knew more about her Indian people. Osages came from every part of the reservation to see her. There were even some visitors from other Oklahoma tribes.

That night, in the Tall Chief Theater owned by her father, Maria was given her name. She was dressed in a lovely Osage costume. On her head was placed a crown of beadwork. To further show their identification with the world outside of the reservation, the Osages gave Maria the title of Princess. She was probably the first Osage princess in history. The applause and Indian whoops rang to the rafters.

It was a highlight in her life. No ovation from any audience anywhere, or yet to come, gave her any greater happiness or feeling of pride than that of the Osages.

Honors continued to pour in. The Governor of Oklahoma made her a colonel on his staff. She was named "Woman of the Year" by the Women's National Press Club. She was awarded the Indian Achievement Award, a national Indian recognition. She was named to the Oklahoma Hall of Fame.

There were many others, and Maria received them all with a kind of wondering joy. Then, for the second time in her life, she went through troubled times over the failure of her marriage.

When she remarried, she had hoped to keep her life as a ballerina separate from her life as a wife. She forgot that she had once reasoned that each was important but should be taken one at a time. Again, she proved herself right. Elmourza Natirboff had no interest in her career, or in ballet. He had no understanding of how important it was to her, of how important she was to her world. To him,

*Mrs. Tall Chief with
Marjorie (left) and Maria*

Maria's dancing was something of a hobby, something she could give up at any time for his plans. When her dancing interfered with what he wanted to do, he became angry. He demanded that she give it up, or he would give her up. It was useless to reason with him. Maria made her choice. She could not stop dancing at this point in her life. So the marriage ended.

Maria was more sharply affected by this breakup than she had been with the one with Balanchine, bitter though it was. She had adored Balanchine as she had adored her other teachers. With him, there had always been a master-pupil relationship, even as man and wife. When no longer man and wife, this relationship continued. She wasn't cut completely adrift.

With the loss of her second husband, Maria grieved deeply. She was emotionally drained and empty. The void in her life was almost more than she could bear.

Gradually she fought her way back to normalcy. She forced herself to shut out the sadness and to rise above the trouble that could have defeated her. However, her experience with deep sorrow and pain had both healed and changed her. Gone was her youth, her dependence on her parents, her teachers, on Balanchine. She rededicated herself to her art as a woman. She had become a woman in every sense of the word.

Where once she had been merely regal, she was now royal. There was a quality in her face and manner that gave her a new dimension of nobility. Because she had gained such emotional depth and understanding, there was no role, now, that she could not dance. She had known happiness and unhappiness, love and the loss of love. She had gone through it all and emerged a much stronger and finer person, a much finer dancer. So she stood at this crossroads in her life.

Balanchine had been watching her. His sensitivity was part of his genius and he sensed what was taking place in Maria. He was quick to seize on it. She was ready, now, for a role that he had once dreamed she would play. He told her that she would be the Sugar Plum Fairy in *The Nutcracker*. She would be the most ravishing Sugar Plum Fairy of all time, he predicted.

This role is considered by ballet experts to be the most difficult of all. The success of the ballet depends entirely upon the ballerina. If she cannot win an audience to believe in the "unbelievable" of the fairy tale, the entire ballet will fail. The Balanchine version of *The Nutcracker* was always presented at Christmas. It had been delighting children and their parents since it was first given in 1954. It was a Balanchine masterpiece and Maria put her heart and soul into the part. Not this time for Balanchine, however, but for herself.

Again, a new Tallchief emerged. Her performance reached a new high and left no doubt in anybody's mind that she was an established prima ballerina.

After this, Maria toured this country with Ballet Russe, the company that had first started her on her career. Audiences everywhere were eager to see her. Her performances were sold out far in advance of the date they were to be given. It was five years since she had toured the country with Ballet Theatre. Now she was one of the most beautiful of all ballerinas. She was of such grace and ability that no one could ever go beyond her, or even equal her. So great was her appeal that she received the highest salary ever paid to any ballerina, $2,000 a week.

Every one of her performances was new and vivid. She was an actress-dancer and could move her watchers to tears or to any other emotional response. She made every performance entirely hers, then and forever after. No one else could be compared to her. She stood alone.

In this country, Maria played in more than one hundred cities. In some, motorcycle policemen had to clear a path for her through the crowds. She had become a living legend.

After the exciting United States tour, Maria returned to the New York City Ballet. She had to get ready at once for a European tour where audiences waited eagerly to see her, too. American ballet lovers wanted to see her because they claimed her as truly theirs. Europeans also wanted to see her as an American, but for a different reason. Could an American, an American Indian, at that, be such a wonderfully great prima ballerina as reported? After all, ballet was a European art.

They had to acknowledge that she was. Her appearances were unqualifiedly glorious, the critics said. All doubts were cast aside. She was not just an American prima ballerina, it was said. She was international. She was peerless, better than any of their favorites. The Europeans took Maria to their hearts.

From then on, Maria went wherever she was asked to dance. She appeared in South America, Canada, Japan, and the Middle East. No adjectives could be found to describe her. How could something so incredibly lovely and so artistically mature be described? Maria Tallchief was the queen of ballet.

CHAPTER IX

A Life
Fulfilled

For some time, Maria's life was a travel pano-
rama. She performed continuously, she was admired constantly. She lived in a goldfish bowl of attention and public
gaze. Such a life is exciting for awhile, but it can grow to
be exhausting. Now and again, Maria found herself longing
for home.

Once more she was in love. She had found the kind of
love that she wanted and needed, but which so far had
eluded her. Her first husband loved Maria Tallchief, the
dancer, clay to be molded. Her second husband loved
Maria, the girl in the spotlight, as a showpiece.

Henry D. Paschen, Jr., a businessman who lived in
Chicago, was her third love. He had great understanding
of Maria, as a woman and as an artist. He would have
liked her to give up her dancing. But he realized that, for
awhile, she still needed to dance.

Maria was strongly tempted. It was time that she
should be thinking seriously of a family, if she were ever
to have one. Marjorie had two handsome sons. She still
lived in France and had not entirely forsaken her dancing.

In 1956, Maria and Henry Paschen were married. She
was still with the New York City Ballet, but things were
changed. Balanchine had left to be with his wife who was

stricken with polio. The company had a new director. There were new ways of doing things and new ballets. Neither André Eglevsky or Maria was pleased with the new order. Both decided to leave.

Maria returned to Chicago. While there, she gave birth to a daughter, Elisa Maria. It seemed that she had never known so much joy. Motherhood was the crowning of her life. Her baby was delightful. Her home was a happy haven. But she could not stay in it. She was still obligated to the New York City Ballet and had to return to the company. She did so, although inwardly she had begun to look forward to retirement. No longer did she need to prove herself. She had climbed to the top. Ovations and honors and applause were a matter of course. No longer was dancing so much of an emotional need. Emotional needs were now fulfilled with love and tenderness and a child.

For Maria's partner, the company had engaged Erik Bruhn. A Dane, he was well-built, blonde, and blue-eyed. His Viking looks were in sharp contrast to Maria's dark beauty. In their dancing together, they were declared the greatest partners in ballet history.

After a short time, both left the New York City Ballet to tour Europe and Russia with the American Ballet Theatre. As usual, audiences worshiped them. The Russians never ceased to marvel that an American could so beautifully embrace the ballet form of the Russian imperial tradition.

More and more, Maria was dancing highly dramatic roles which set forth her abilities as a fine actress. When she returned to New York, she was cast to appear in *Miss Julie*, a ballet based on a tragic play.

As soon as this was announced, there was a rush to buy tickets. What would Tallchief do with this role? The story was about a young woman of good family who was caught in an unfortunate love affair. Step by step, she sank through degradation. In the end she commits suicide.

Maria gave of her utmost. She was haughty, passionate, and despairing. Miss Julie became a real person instead of a character on a stage. When she died, the audience wept in sympathy. Once more, Maria had surpassed herself.

Walter Terry, one of the best of the New York critics, spoke for everyone. "What can one say when faced with the closest to perfection that dancing mortals can achieve," he wrote. There could be no greater praise than that.

When one has reached the stars, where else is there to go? Maria had danced in every corner of the world and in almost every country. Her years of hard work and sacrifice were rewarded with the success and approval given to only a very few. She had everything that she could possibly want — fame and honor as a dancer, respect as a person, praise and admiration in full measure.

The time had come to say good-bye while she was still at her best. The time had come to leave when she would be long remembered. A new life awaited in Chicago.

In 1966, the ballet shoes were put away for the last time. There was no feeling of sadness, no lingering desire. Again she had made her choice. There were no regrets.

In Chicago, Maria lives in a lovely home on the city's north side. She also has a beautiful home in the suburb of Highland Park. And life continues to be exciting, for she is a leader in Chicago society and gives prominent help to civic affairs and benefit programs.

One of Maria's interests is opera and she is teaching new apprentices of the Chicago Civic Opera Company in the aesthetics of dancing. She serves also on the Woman's Board of the Opera Company.

Maria is active in Indian affairs and has assisted the local Indian Center on various occasions. She is a director of Indian Council Fire Achievement Award, Inc., which presents the annual Indian Achievement Award. One of her sister Marjorie's twin sons has now entered law school, and she is delighted over this, looking forward to the time when he may be able to help Indian people through his legal skills, for such help is badly needed.

But ballet is still Maria's major interest, and it is in this field that most of her activities lie. She speaks of a time when there might be a Chicago ballet company, and if she can have a part in bringing this about, she most certainly will. Also, she is engaged in teaching and lecturing, traveling across the country to appear before college classes and groups where The Dance is part of the fine arts curriculum. She also participates in Indian cultural studies and seminars sponsored by colleges and universities. Her busy schedule includes frequent appearances on educational television programs.

Since her retirement, Maria has received a number of honorary doctorates — one from Colby College, one from Lake Forest College, one from Ripon College, and a distinguished service award from the University of Oklahoma. She has also received a number of other outstanding awards, among them the Cappezio Dance Award, the award of the National Institute of Arts and Letters, and others. She had the honor to be chosen one of the Legendary Women of

America, and other recognitions will continue to come. For Maria Tallchief has brought luster to American ballet and placed it on an equal footing with the ballet standards of the European countries that first nurtured the art, and she will remain an ideal and example for generations of dancers to come.

Maria's daughter Elisa is a charming child, somewhat resembling her mother, but fair-haired. Watching Elisa grow is one of her mother's delights. Elisa studies ballet but is not much interested in it. Her love is music, and she is a talented pianist, carrying on this other talent of her mother's that found expression only in her childhood. She is also a very good student, a happy, well-adjusted youngster, friendly and not at all shy.

When Maria speaks of her gifted child's future, she says the choice of a career will be Elisa's. Should she choose ballet, she will know that it is a terribly lonely life and a very demanding one. It is a life in which career will have to be placed above everything else and even with hard work the gains will be uncertain. How well Maria Tallchief knows the story!

Maria, Elisa, and Henry Paschen
at home in Chicago

THE AUTHOR

Marion E. Gridley, author of more
than twenty published books on American
Indian subjects, is an adopted member
of the Omaha and Winnebago tribes.
Since 1952 she has published *The
Amerindian,* a bimonthly periodical for
and about American Indians.

*The photographs are reproduced through
the courtesy of the New York City
Ballet, Oklahoma Historical Society,
Maria Tallchief Paschen, and Mrs.
Ruth Tall Chief.*

OTHER BIOGRAPHIES
IN THIS SERIES ARE